D. D Kelly

The Principles of Free Trade

As Shown by Gladstone, Wells, Perry, Sumner, And Others

D. D Kelly

The Principles of Free Trade
As Shown by Gladstone, Wells, Perry, Sumner, And Others

ISBN/EAN: 9783744734035

Printed in Europe, USA, Canada, Australia, Japan

Cover: Foto ©ninafisch / pixelio.de

More available books at **www.hansebooks.com**

AS SHOWN BY

MESSRS. GLADSTONE, WELLS, PERRY, SUMNER, AND OTHERS.

THIS PAMPHLET IS PUBLISHED ONLY FOR THE
PURPOSE OF SHOWING TO THOSE
WHO DESIRE TO KNOW,

THAT OUR PRESENT TARIFF IS A SWINDLE

UPON THE GREAT MASS OF OUR PEOPLE.

——————————

EAST BOSTON:
WM. B. MORSE, PRINTER.
1886.

To THE CITIZENS OF BOSTON:

In presenting this pamphlet to the public I do so with the desire that the mechanic, laborer and business man, who has a desire, can learn from some of the ablest writers of the day the principle of free trade. These papers will all be found to be able and positive: no chance for misunderstanding each. Of those who have kindly contributed to this publication, some of the speeches and writings have been delivered some two or three years, particularly so of Mr. Gladstone's; and I here commend this address of Mr. Gladstone to your attention as having four-fold the bearing and effect on our country to that of his. Some of the letters which I publish have no doubt been read before, but have not been freely distributed to our people.

In old times the Democratic and Whig parties were so patriotic, and each had so much faith in their principles, that they furnished the means to give to the young man the opportunity of learning the principles of political economy by courses of public lectures. On the Democratic side we had able men, among them no more able than Robert Rantoul. The leaders of our old party in those days were not office-seekers, but men who were devoted to the cause from principle alone. Then to our papers we looked for able editorials on the tariff; to-day we look for them, and find in their place base-ball, billiard games, or notice of some mill, as they call it, between two inhuman beasts that meet to mash each other's face.

The only speeches which we obtain from our so-called leaders are given after dinner, and generally the information obtained is very foggy. And so the work of informing the young is left to chance, and what little may be done by the Free Trade Club of Boston.

And hence this all-important question which concerns the bread of every man, that should demand the attention of all statesmen and men of thought, has not an able advocate in the ranks of the Democratic party in this State who has the manly pluck to take a stand against the monopolists who ask the millions to contribute to their already too much ill-gotten gains.

Kidd took ship, cargo, and often life. We are told this was against the law, but our ships arrive to-day and by some legalized law, made by Kelly, Randall, and others, you rob them of but 60 per cent., which, in other words, is simply lawful plunder of the few against the many.

All I ask is, to read with care the evidence given you, and then pass the pamphlet to your neighbor.

D. D. KELLY.

HOW DO THEY LIKE IT THEMSELVES?

BY PROF. A. L. PERRY.

The real opinion of the leading protectionists of the United States in regard to the nature and effect of "protective" tariff-taxes is precisely the same as the opinion of the free traders. If one should listen to the words only of the protectionists, he might indeed infer that their opinions were diametrically opposed to those of the others in respect to the whole operation of tariff-taxes; but it is not wise nor safe to judge of their opinions by their words alone on a point like this; like all other men, protectionists are to be tested in practical matters by their actions as well as by their words, and by their actions much more than by their words; and when they are judged by this common-sense and universal rule, namely, that actions speak louder than words, it is found to a demonstration that they estimate the effect of tariff-taxes in raising the price of domestic goods exactly as the free traders estimate it.

Indeed a further distinction needs to be drawn even in respect to the words used by protectionists, according to the place and time when and where the words are employed, according to whether they are talking to their neighbors and employees at home or to the members of the Committee of Ways and Means at Washington. A striking change of language has often been observed in the mouth of protectionists according to a change in the audience, and according to whether they wanted to get something new and better for themselves in the way of legislation, or whether they were trying to account for and justify to outsiders what had already been done at their instance. The words of protectionists when they talk to one another and when they talk or write to the Ways and Means Committee, are ten times as significant of their true opinions, and agree ten times more nearly with the opinions of free traders than when they talk or write for "Buncombe." For example, when the Bessemer steel men sent their now famous circular to the Ways and Means Committee in 1870, marking it as "confidential," and asking in it for two cents a pound tariff-tax on foreign steel rails, they admitted in it in so many words that they expected to supply wholly the domestic demand for steel rails, consequently the government would not get a penny from the tariff-tax, but the domestic rails would be raised in price to consumers $44.80 a ton. Their opinion and action and expectation corresponded precisely with the view of free traders as to the purpose and effect of "protective" tariff-taxes; as was in fact illustrated by the tax of one and one quarter cents a pound, or $28 a ton, granted to the companies on steel rails by the Committee and then by Congress shortly after.

The simple truth is, and I am going now to demonstrate it by unquestionable facts, that our protectionists like very much to have their neighbors and fellow-countrymen pay "protective" tariff-taxes, especially the large classes of them like the farmers and the wages-takers, *but they do not like to pay such taxes themselves, and never will pay them if they can escape it either by hook or by crook :* thus confessing by unmistakable action that their real opinion about such taxes is just the same as that of the free traders.

The first example of this that comes to mind is that of Samuel Williston and his partners engaged in the manufacture of buttons for many years in the village of Easthampton, Massachusetts. The information on this point came directly to me from one of the superintendents of the mill, and also from one of the citizens of the village of high character and high position. Indeed the facts, as I shall now state them, have long been well known in Western Massachusetts, and equally well known in the Customs service of the United States. These gentlemen were strong protectionists ; they talked it to their laborers, they talked it to their fellow-villagers, and, what is more to the point, they secured in favor of their own finished buttons a "protective" tariff-tax of the heaviest against foreign buttons of that class—a tax that still subsists. The sole purpose of this tax was to keep out of the home market competing for-

eign buttons. and to raise the price of their own buttons artificially and proportionally to the price of the foreign with
the taxes added. They secured this in precisely the same way
that every "protective" tariff-tax has been secured in this country from 1789 to this hour. namely. by personal instance and
pressure brought to bear upon the Committee of Ways and
Means. and by log-rolling with other interests that had a similar end in view.

Very well. They obtained protectionism for themselves and
liked it very much. To be sure, all their neighbors and all their
fellow-countrymen had to pay in consequence a largely enhanced price for their buttons, but that only concerned them as
it increased, just as it was designed to increase, their own
profits. But, unluckily for them as protectionists. they had to
buy foreign cloth with which to cover their buttons, that had
been burdened by a heavy duty under the same impulse and
even in the same bill as had "protected" their own finished buttons. This was not so pleasant, to pay artificially enhanced
prices on their material. But if protectionism was good for the
country and for the button-makers, it must have been by the
same reasoning good for the country and for the cloth-makers.
Sauce for the goose is sauce for the gander. But Mr. Williston and company immediately confessed in action that they
were not protectionists, except so far as the scheme brought
grist to their own mill ; they at once acknowledged emphatic-
ally that the free traders are right in their view of the action
of tariff-taxes in raising prices ; and they gave orders that the
foreign cloth bought for their mill to cover buttons with,
should be slit and cut so as to come in at the custom house
as " damaged goods," and so escape the " protective " tariff-
taxes designed to raise the price of domestic cloth. Slitting
and cutting did not harm the cloth one penny for their purposes, but it enabled them to get off scot-free of tariff-taxes.
*They did not like to pay protective tariff-taxes. and escaped
them by a subterfuge.*

Later they practised an ingenious device. by which their
own manufacture was forwarded. and their escape from the
taxes secured at the same time. A circular gouge cutting out

bits of cloth-circles just big enough to cover each a button, was struck down over and over again through the pieces of cloth before shipment, and the perforated piece and the circles cut out of it still passed muster at the custom house as "damaged goods." This they did in one form or another for years and years; the government frequently protested and struggled, but the button-makers carried the day every time by precisely the same influences as they had gotten their protectionism at first. Doubtless they meant to be honorable men and good citizens, and in fact they were "not sinners above all the Galileans because they did such things": but their action was perfectly conclusive as to what they thought about protectionism in general, about taxes that they had *to pay*, about the scheme as a whole of swindling the many for the benefit of the few.

The next instance that comes to mind is that of Erastus B. Bigelow, of Boston, and his confederates and subordinates in the carpet industry, which was and is a highly "protected" industry. Mr. Bigelow was an honorable man and a good citizen, and deserved the highest credit for his ingenuity and success as an inventor of carpet machinery, on which he had valuable patents. He called himself a protectionist, and was so regarded by his neighbors; the writer remembers to have seen him cuddled very close to Horace Greeley on the stage of Music Hall, in Boston, on the occasion of a memorable tariff-debate, in which Greeley took part, in October, 1868; but he was not a protectionist certainly when it came to tariff taxes on the raw material of his own industry, wool; because his sentiments as expressed in repeated and emphatic action corresponded precisely so far forth with the convictions and actions of all intelligent free traders.

On August 10, 1866, a supplemental tariff-act went into operation, enacted solely for the sake of increasing "protective" tariff-taxes without seeming to do so, that provided that the costs of freight, shipment, commission, brokerage, and all similar charges, should be added to the invoice value of imports to make up the custom house value on which the taxes should be levied. This increase of protectionism applied to all dutiable imports whatsoever "*except to long-combing or carpet wools costing twelve cents or less per pound.*" Why this single exception? Why could not the carpet-manufacturers pay tariff-taxes as well as all other people? No person in the United States could buy a carpet without paying prices enormously increased for their sole benefit; and yet they were unwilling to pay, and successfully resisted paying, a comparatively slight increase of taxes applied to all other dutiable things without exception!

It could not be that the carpet industry was then depressed, and this remarkable exemption happened on that account, because, ten days before this law went into effect, the Hartford Carpet Company declared *a semi-annual dividend of twenty per centum*, and its $100 shares were worth $275 dividend off.

Being a Yankee and wanting to know, you know, I asked Mr. Dawes shortly after, who was then representative from this congressional district, how this extraordinary exception was brought about, and who the man was who had accomplished it. His reply was: " *You really know just as much about that as I know. All I know is, that in the first and second readings of the bill that clause was not in it; between the second and third readings, the exception was inserted, and the bill passed so. I believe Mr. Bigelow was in Washington at the time.*"

This was in 1866. The next year passed the famous Wool and Woollens Tariff, which was a compromise and log-roll between the wool-growers and the woollen-manufacturers, largely mediated by Mr. Bigelow. The manufacturers had gotten in the usual way high taxes on foreign cloth, and liked very much the resulting high prices of their domestic cloth; but they stood in great fear lest the wool-growers should follow their example and go to Washington and get wool "protected" also. They *bought* wool, while they *sold* cloth. They agreed with the free traders perfectly, so far as wool was concerned, that it is a blessed thing to buy in the cheapest market. They poor-pussied the wool-growers, they cajoled them, they even menaced them when the latter began to demand protectionism for wool. These could

not see why wool was not as much entitled to an artificial price as woollens. Vermont and Ohio spoke in
louder and louder tones, till at last the wool-growers of these
and other States said to the manufacturers of cloth in words of
downright business: "*You accord to us the same privileges
that you have under the law or you will lose your own!*"

Then followed the compromise of 1867. The wool and
woollens tariff of that year was a public and conspicuous confession of the truth, which free traders have always maintained,
that the sole design and the actual result of protectionism is to
raise the price of domestic products at the expense of the
masses, without the least reference to the wants of the national
treasury. The manufacturers staved off the growers till the
last possible moment, like very free traders, and proclaimed
thereby how admirable a thing it is to buy in a free market;
and when compelled to surrender their free raw material to
burdensome taxes for the sake of the wool-growers, they confessed the effect of such taxes (just as the free traders allege it)
by raising anew the duties that "protected" themselves by as
much as they supposed the wool would be raised by the
tariff-taxes accorded now for the first time to the wool-growers.
Mr. Bigelow saw to it, that under the new arrangement long-
combing and carpet wool should still come in from abroad
under a very slight tariff-tax, while all other wools came in (if
at all) under a very heavy tax, alleging in excuse, that *such
carpet wool was not produced in the United States, and
therefore did not need "protecting;"* and so gave in
again his emphatic testimony in action to the undoubted benefits of free trade. If such wool as he used for raw material
were not grown in the United States, then every dollar of tax
upon it would have redounded wholly to the benefit of the
Treasury of the United States; but, like all other protectionists as such, he cared nothing for the revenue of his country;
since every "protective" tariff-tax whatsoever *is designed to
prevent revenue* by keeping the articles taxed out of the country in whole or in part.

My present purpose does not allow me to explain, which
could be very easily done, why it is, that the wool and wool-

lens tariff of 1867 has kept both the main parties to it, the growers and the manufacturers, in the slough of despond ever since.

The third instance of the remarkable fact, to which attention is now called, turns on John B. Alley, of Lynn, Mass. My informant at this point also is Mr. Dawes, whose own sense of humor is quite too keen not to enjoy more or less the ridiculous spot into which he himself and his fellow-protectionists are thrown by zealous confession in spots, that the free traders are all right. *"I do not wonder,"* said Mr. Dawes, *"that men who think as you do make a mockery of us protectionists."* Mr. Alley was a protectionist with the rest in 1867. He thought it was a good plan for the farmers and the laborers and all other folks that used American cloth to pay an extra price for it for the benefit of the manufacturers. But he did *not* think it was a good plan for his neighbors and friends and constituents in Lynn, the busy shoemakers, to pay an artificial price under protectionism for their lastings and webbings, a part of the raw material of their trade. These shoemakers had sent him to Congress repeatedly, and might do it again ; and besides, he saw that it would be a great discouragement to the trade of the town if these raw materials of shoes were doubled in price by the tariff, or even increased 75 *per centum*. He read an incidental description in the tariff-bill, which he feared would cover these lastings and webbings ; and he started for Washington at once, only to meet in New York the adjourned New England members, who had already passed the bill, and killed the shoemakers undesignedly.

Poor Mr. Alley! He went back to Lynn a sadder and a wiser man. It makes a great difference with protectionists, does it not? Whether they themselves or their friends or their constituents are compelled to pay the enhanced prices caused by protectionism, or whether the general public are to pay them, of whom they know nothing and care less.

The last instance of this sort of thing is the most striking and the most shameless of all. In October, 1871, Chicago was burned down to the ground. The whole country, and the whole world, were startled by the catastrophe. As Whittier puts it in ever-living lines:

"A sudden impulse thrilled each wire
That signalled round that sea of fire:
Sweet words of cheer, warm heart-throbs came;
In tears of pity died the flame!

From East and West, from South and North,
The messages of hope shot forth:
And, underneath the severing wave,
The world, full-handed, reached to save."

But could not Congress do something for the ruined city? They met two months afterward, and some one proposed a bill remitting " protective " tariff-taxes on building materials for one year only and for the benefit of Chicago alone. What a wholesale confession of the real effect of protectionism is here! What a free trade measure in spirit and scope was that proposed! The national bounty to the people of a great city in ruins was to take the form of allowing them to get the materials for rebuilding their town for one year only at their natural price—as cheap as they could be had in the free markets of the world. That was well. And it was a great and public acknowledgement in the face of mankind of the true purpose and the actual result of protectionism on the prices of some of the necessaries of life to the masses of their fellow-countrymen. For a moment the majority of Congress entered into the needs and the feelings of those who are compelled in poverty and misfortune to pay artificially high prices for the bare necessaries of life under protectionism. In a spasm of virtuous sympathy with the unfortunate Congress asked themselves, How should we like it ourselves in like circumstances? This was free trade doctrine. This was a broad confession on the positive side.

But listen now. Hear a shrieking confession of the same truth on the negative side. The lumber lords of Michigan and Wisconsin were astonished to hear that Congress proposed to interfere with their artificial profits on lumber, extorted by law out of their fellow-citizens, even for one year, even for the partial relief of the unfortunates of Chicago ; and a parlor car, filled with some of these greedy monopolists, was rolled to Washington in haste ; and lo ! the bill of relief, as passed by Congress and signed by the President, *excepted lumber* from the proposed remission of tariff-taxes on building materials for one year for the sole benefit of Chicago ! Read the shameful story in U. S. Statutes for 1872, page 33. This transaction, perhaps better than any other in its history, discloses the inmost nature and the very animating spirit of protectionism. From one case learn all. It cares nothing for the rights of men, nothing for the needs of the poor, nothing for decency even, nothing for righteousness, and nothing for the wrath of God.

WILLIAMS COLLEGE. Feb. 1, 1886.

BROAD PRINCIPLES UNDERLYING THE TARIFF CONTROVERSY.

BY PROF. W. G. SUMNER, OF YALE COLLEGE.

A Lecture delivered before the International Free Trade Alliance.

The world has heard a great deal about liberty for the last century. That period has been marked by great struggles on the part of nations to secure independence, and on the part of classes and individuals to secure freedom from old traditional restraints. The world has struggled towards "freedom" and "liberty" as if these were the first considerations of peace, justice, prosperity and happiness, and the result has been to produce, in the forefront of modern civilization, states whose fundamental principle is to give the freest scope to individual energy and effort.

We in the United States make it our greatest boast that we have accepted this broad principle absolutely, and applied it fearlessly ; nevertheless, we, who are met here to-night, are associated to demand more liberty. There is no body of our fellow-citizens worth mentioning who deny the right and the expediency of private property. What we have to demand, and what the majority of our fellow citizens—so far as their will as yet been constitutionally expressed—deny us, is the privilege of using our property as we like, that is, of exchanging it when and where and with whomsoever we will. When we demand this privilege, which belongs to us on the simplest principles of right reason and common sense, we are met by a speculative theory based on artificial assumptions, put forward sometimes on bare considerations of selfish interest, and sometimes with no little parade of abstract philosophising. We are told, "Oh, no ! It is not best for the state that you should do as you like about making your exchanges. The legislature must consider the question, and prescribe for you with whom and for what you shall exchange. If you deal with the designated persons, your countrymen, they will gain, the wealth of the community will increase, and you, as a member of the community, will participate, and be better off in the end than if you had been let alone."

Now, we dispute this theory at every stage. We deny that the state, *i.e.*, the legislature, can make any such provision for us better than we can make for ourselves, and we appeal to experience of everything it tries to do: we deny that it has any business to theorize for us in the premises; we deny that the designated persons will gain—at least, that they will gain as much as they would if they were left to deal with us on their own footing; we deny that they can gain anything from us, *on account of the law*, but what we lose; we deny that the total gains to one part of society by this process can ever exceed the total losses by another part, *i.e.*, that the process can increase the wealth of the community; we deny, finally, that our share of these hypothetical gains can ever be redistributed to us so as to bring back our first loss. We have never seen money go through such a process, passing through many hands, and come back whole, to say nothing of loss and waste.

Thus the issue is joined. On the one side are broad and simple principles, so elementary that they are mere truisms, and on the other side are special pleas of various kinds set up to befog men's judgment, and prevent them from drawing the inferences which follow inevitably.

Let me suggest to you two or three of the broadest and most commanding principles which really decide this question:

1. We, Americans, have made it the first principle of our society that no man shall obtain by law any advantage in the race of life on account of birth or rank, or any traditional or fictitious privilege of any kind whatsoever, and on the other hand, we have removed, so far as the law can remove, all the hindrances and stumbling blocks which come from circumstances of birth and family. Society gives no aid, but it removes all obstacles of social prejudice and tradition. There is not a man in the country who does not respond with a full

heart to the wisdom and truth of this relation of society to the individual. Now, on what principle is this relation based? It is on the belief that society makes the most of its members in that way. Some men have more in them than others. We do not know which is which until they show it; but we believe that the way to let each one come to his best, is for society to set them all on their feet, and then let them run each for himself. We believe that the best powers of the community are brought out in that way.

It does not follow that men so treated never make mistakes, and never ruin themselves. We see them do this every day; but if it were proposed that the state should interfere, few would be led astray by the proposition.

The same principle applies to trade directly and completely. The productive powers of men and communities differ, but whatever they are, more or less, they reach their maximum under liberty. The total of national wealth is greatest where each disposes of his own energy in production and exchange with the least interference. This is not saying that none will make mistakes, or that free trade will eliminate all ills from human life. Free trade will not make the idle enjoy the fruits of industry, nor the thriftless possess the rewards of economy. Poverty, pain, disease, misery will remain as long as idleness and vice remain. Free trade will only act in its own measure and way, to leave men face to face with these things, with a somewhat better chance to conquer them. It is one of the great vices of protection that it makes the industrious suffer for the idle, and the energetic and enterprising bear the losses of the stupid.

2. If, now, you examine the opposite theory you will find that it assumes that we or our ancestors all made a great mistake in coming to this country and trying to live here. We are told that a tariff is necessary to "make a market" for our farmers, that a tariff is necessary to keep our manufactures from destruction, that navigation laws are necessary to preserve our shipping. Some of the old countries support a population twenty or thirty times as dense as ours with little

or nothing of this artificial system. If, then, we are not able to
live here without this aid, we must have left a part of the world
where life is easier for one where it is harder. This brings
me, then,

3. To the great fundamental error of the theory, viz. : That
taxation is a productive force. No emigrants go to the desert
of Sahara. None would go to New York if it were sand and
rocks. If, however, New York is a part of the earth's surface,
consisting of arable land fit to produce food for man ; if it is
intersected by mountains, covered by forests, and containing
iron and coal, and if it possesses great rivers and a splendid har-
bor, then the conditions of supporting human life are fulfilled.
It requires only labor and capital to build up there a great and
prosperous community. It is plain that some parts of the
earth's surface contain more materials for man's use than others,
and the fact as to New York will affect the wealth of its in-
habitants. It is plain that it makes a difference whether the
people are idle or industrious, listless or energetic, sluggish or
enterprising. It is plain that it makes a difference how much
capital they have, or whether there are enough of them for the
best distribution of labor. It is plain that it makes a difference
what is the state of the arts and sciences, and what are the
facilities for transportation.

The wealth of New York at any given time must depend on
the way in which these factors are combined. Now the
question arises : How can taxation possibly increase the product? Which one of the factors does it act upon?

Just consider what taxation is. We pay taxes, in the first
place, to pay for the necessary organization of society, in order
that we may act together, and not at cross purposes like a mob ;
but if that were all the state had to do taxes would be very
small. We must support courts and police, and army and
navy. These we need for peace, and justice, and security.
But suppose that there were none who had the will to rob, or
to swindle, or to cheat, or to do violence, the expenditures
under this head would dwindle to nothing. It follows that
taxes are the tribute we pay to avarice, and violence, and
rapine and all the other vices which disfigure human nature.

Taxes are only those evils translated into money and spread over the community. They are so much taken from the strength of the laborer, or the fertility of the soil, or the benefit of the climate. They are loss and waste to almost their entire extent.

This is the function of government then, which it is proposed to use to create value, to do what men can do only by applying labor and capital to land. Let us take a case to test it. Let us suppose that no woollen cloth is made in New York, but that a New York farmer, at the end of a certain time has ten bushels of wheat, of which one bushel will buy a yard of imported cloth. After the exchange then he has nine bushels of wheat and one yard of cloth. If any one could make cloth in New York as easily as he could raise a bushel of wheat, some one would do it as soon as there was unemployed labor and capital, and that would be the end of the matter; but if no one undertakes the business it must be because labor and capital are all employed, or because it takes more labor and capital to produce a yard of cloth than a bushel of wheat. Let us suppose that it would take as much as a bushel and a half of wheat. Now, a protectionist proposes to the state to tax imported cloth one-half bushel of wheat per yard. If his plan is carried out the difficulty of obtaining imported cloth is raised to one bushel and a half of wheat per yard, which is the rate of difficulty at which it can be produced in New York. The protectionist then begins and offers his cloth at a bushel and a half per yard. The farmer who, as before, has produced ten bushels, now buys at the new rate, and after the exchange stands possessed of eight and a half bushels of wheat and one yard of cloth. Whither has the other half bushel gone? It has gone to make up a fund to hire some men to make life in New York harder than God and nature made it. From time to time we are told how much "our industries have increased." So far as their increase is in fact due to this arrangement, it is only a proof how much mischief has been done. This application of taxation does not alter the nature of taxation, it only extends its effects arbitrarily and needlessly, and inflicts upon the people a greater measure than they need otherwise bear of the burden which is due to robbery, injustice, war, famine and the other social ills.

4. Protection is, moreover, hostile to improvements. We are always eager to devise improved methods and to invent machinery to "save labor," and every such improvement which we introduce involves the waste and destruction of a great deal of capital. Old machinery must be discarded, although it is not worn out. This loss is not incurred by anybody willingly ; it is enforced by competition. When, therefore, competition is withdrawn or limited the incentive to improvement is lessened or destroyed. This applies especially in manufactures where the international competition is cut off by protective duties. The same principle that protection resists improvement applies even more distinctly to those improvements which are made in transportation. In spite of their theories men rejoice in all the improved means of communication which bring nations nearer together. A new railroad or an improved steamship is regarded as a step gained in civilization. Such improvements are realized in diminished freights and diminished prices of imported goods. No sooner is this realized, however, than "foreign competition" is found to be worse than ever. An outcry goes up for "more protection," and a new tax is put on to-day to counteract what we rejoiced over yesterday as an immense gain. We spend millions to dredge out our harbors, to remove rocks and cut channels through sandbars, as if it were a gain to have communication inward and outward as free as possible, and as soon as we experience the effects in reduced cost of goods we lay a new tax, like restoring the sandbars, in order to undo our work. Indeed, to build sandbars across our harbors would be a far cheaper means of reaching the same end. Next, we find that the numerous and complicated taxes have made it impossible for us to build ships to sail across the ocean where they must come in competition with foreign ships ; so we make navigation acts and forbid the purchase of ships, exclude foreigners from our coasting trade, and finally, propose bounties and subsidies, all of which must come at last out of the products of our labor, in order to try to get ships once more. It is like the man who cut a piece from his coat to mend his trowsers, a piece from his vest to replace the hole in his coat, a piece from his trowsers to restore his vest, and so

on over again. Did he ever get a whole suit? He found in a little while that he had only a rag left.

We are told, however, that if we do not do all this we shall be "inundated" with foreign goods. The word is appalling, and carries with it a fallacy which often seems to have great power. On what terms shall we get this flood of good things? Will they be given to us? If so, what can we do better than to stop work and live on this generosity? Why are we, however, selected as the especial objects of this bounty, if bounty it is? Why do not England and France and Belgium and Germany pour out their inundations on Patagonia and Iceland? The answer is plain enough. The goods are not gifts, they are offered for exchange. Nothing can force us to buy or dictate terms of exchange ; and the inundation comes to us because we are known to be rich and able, and because we inhabit a continent prolific in some of the chief objects of human desire. It is not the beggar who, when he goes down the street, is "inundated" with wares from the various stores. If it were he would probably stem the tide with joy. It is the rich man only to whom good things are freely offered with a well understood condition ; few rich men have ever been heard to complain of it. If, then, the Americans have these good things offered them in exchange, and they allow themselves to be worsted in the bargain, they sadly belie their reputation.

These few observations which I have now presented as bearing on the subject are very broad and comprehensive, and very sweeping in their effect. They appeal directly to common sense and right reason. They give us the correct point of view, and dispel some of the fog which has collected from habit and prejudice around this subject. They lead us right up to the doctrine which the United States have put in practice in their own internal trade—absolute freedom of exchange and local or internal taxation. We have proved the practical value of that system here over a continent. I cannot see why the same system would not be a great gain if extended over Canada, Mexico and the West Indies. I cannot see why it would not be a great gain if all South America were embraced in a confederation exactly like ours as far as this point is concerned, with absolute free trade between the states. I cannot see why all Europe would not gain by similar relations, as far as trade is concerned ; and I see no reason why it should not be equally beneficient if extended to the whole civilized globe.

The objections come in the shape of stubborn prejudices and old errors attaching to narrow and special considerations. Some people dread the sweep of a great general principle, however clear and certain and scientific it may be. They dispose of it as a "theory." Well, I am a theorist. I accept the disabilities and demand the advantages of my position ; and when I find a great principle founded in an observation of facts and experience, I am not afraid to follow it up to its last corrollary. The statesman must do what he can in the face of tradition and prejudice and vested interests, and I presume that it will be long before the public will be so enlightened as to demand to feel every cent that it pays in taxes for the very sake of knowing the amount, but I am clear in regard to the wisdom of such an arrangement.

In the further lectures which I am to give I propose to treat the subject historically for I believe that the tariff history of the United States shows most clearly some of the worst of the evils of the system, and I think that every one ought to know how this system has grown up and been fastened upon us.

THE STORY OF THE BESSEMER STEEL MONOPOLY.

BY HON. DAVID A. WELLS.

This story, although often told, embraces, nevertheless, some facts that are not generally known and which cannot too often be repeated to the American public.

In 1855, Henry Bessemer, an Englishman, discovered a new process for making steel. As far as the product was concerned there was not much of novelty in what Mr. Bessemer accomplished, for just as good, and even better steel was made, and made abundantly before. But the great merit of Bessemer's discovery was that it made cheap an article most essential to the progress of civilization, which was before dear. And the whole world rejoiced in the result, as one of the great achievements of the nineteenth century. We say the whole world, but we are mistaken: the United States apparently did not rejoice, for a portion of its people, after waiting until the new discovery had been proved a success, and so avoiding participation in the loss and expense that is always incident to an experiment in manufactures, went to work to neutralize the benefit of Mr. Bessemer's discovery, by depriving it of its special merit—namely, cheapness. And they succeeded in a great degree in so doing, by inducing Congress to impose a duty of nearly 100 per cent. on the import of all Bessemer steel imported from Europe, and then augmenting the price of all steel that was made in this country to an equal or nearly equal extent. It is also to be noted as a further part of this history, that the persons who sought and obtained from Congress the power to tax to such an enormous extent the people and interests of the country who desired to use the new steel—the railroads more especially in the first instance, and then all who used the railroads for freight and travel—had previously acquired by purchase at a very low price the exclusive control of the patent granted to Mr. Bessemer in the United States; and that they then, after being thus doubly fortified against all possible competition at home or from abroad, formed a company or ring, of some eleven associates, and refused to allow any other persons to engage in the manufacture of the new steel, except on condition of paying to the American owners of the patents a royalty so large as to be practically destructive of all profit to all outside parties.

So the business outside of the operations of the eleven associates has not until very lately been in any degree extended. But now that some of the original patents have expired, a few other parties are beginning to engage in the business. The American people, however, by reason of the tariff, are paying all the same as before for their Bessemer steel, or about double the price paid by the people of other countries, their compeers in wealth and civilization.

And how much does the tax at present amount to annually? Let us see. The domestic production of steel rails for the year 1880 was 954,460 net tons; the importations were 158,230 tons, indicating a domestic consumption for the year of 1,112,690 tons. The average prices of the American product for the year 1880 was $67.50. The average prices of Bessemer rails in Great Britain for the same period were between £6 and £7, or from $30 to $35. It is, therefore, clear that the full pound of flesh—$28 per ton—which the tariff allows, was taken on all the Bessemer rails bought and used in the United States during the year 1880, and that this increment of price in consequence—which was a tax on domestic consumption—amounted in the aggregate to $31,155,320. *Thirty-one millions of dollars!!!* Truly a big sum! A sum so large that the mind is unable to take its measure except by instituting comparisons, or finding out how much the same number of dollars will buy of some other commodities. Let us, therefore, as a help to mental comprehension, institute some of these tests or comparisons. Thus if a man were to attempt to count this sum at the rate of a dollar a second, it would take him more than a year, working twenty-four hours a day, or more than two years at twelve hours a day to do it. It represents more than three times the net ordinary expenditures of the entire federal government in the year 1880, and more than half the ordinary expenditures of the government during the last year of Buchanan's administration. The fishery business of the great lakes is an extensive and laborious branch of domestic industry, giving employment in 1880 to 5,050 men, and supplying the country with a most desirable and cheap article of food. And yet, taking the value of the catch for 1880 ($17,84,050) as the basis for estimate, these 5,050 poor and industrious men would be required to work and give the entire product of their work for more than seventeen years in order to raise money enough to pay the tax which the tariff at present imposes annually on the entire people and industries of the country for the benefit of comparatively very few people, and for one single branch of domestic industry. And out of this great tax of $31,155,320, only $4,479,236 passed into the national treasury. Again, if we assume the average product of wheat in the United States at fifteen bushels per acre, and that the farmer receives on the average one dollar per bushel gross for his product—both not unfair assumptions—and further that the bounty to the steel rail manufacturers, [which accrued directly to their profit in 1880, by reason of the tariff, had been paid to them in wheat in place of money; or, to put the case still differently, if we suppose the American steel rail makers to have sold their products in 1880 at the same price as their European competitors were glad to sell—from $30 to $35 per ton—and then that the federal government, with a view of rewarding their struggling patriotic efforts, had sent out its revenue officials, who arbitrarily took from the farmers and delivered to the steel rail makers twenty-eight bushels of wheat for every ton which they manufactured and sold; it would have required 26,724,800 bushels, (more than was grown in 1880 in the entire State of Wisconsin, Missouri or Kansas) or the product of 1,781,658 acres to have given them an equivalent in value to the bounty which they actually received in money during the same year, under the existing tariff.

Now it is not pretended that these steel rail taxes are paid primarily or exclusively from the products of the fisheries, or from the crops of the farmers—although the burden does rest in a great degree upon the latter, who furnish the bulk of the commodities transported by rail ; but as all taxes, of whatever name and nature, must be paid out of the products of labor, and can be paid from no other fund, then somebody, in order to pay the enhanced cost of the domestic consumption of steel rails, over and above what passed into the federal treasury, must have performed a service equal to growing 26,724,880 bushels of wheat or of cultivating 1,781,658 acres of land. And for this enormous amount of labor the toilers were in no way benefitted, for they might have sold all the products of their labor for the same price as they did receive, and have had an exemption in addition from the tax, to represent profits or surplus in their pockets.

We have here, therefore, an illustration in the nature of a demonstration of the manner in which protection interferes with the natural distribution of wealth ; enriching the few at the cost of the many.

But this record of the greed and rapacity of the steel rail manufacturers of the United States is not yet complete. Not content with the exclusive ownership of the patent right to manufacture : not satisfied with the exactment of an exorbitant tariff on the import of all competing products, they sought and obtained from Congress, in conjunction with the iron manufacturers, the right to forcibly compel the purchase of these commodities by certain great domestic consumers. Thus they would not consent to the granting of charters by the government to the several Pacific railroads, even when the construction of these roads was regarded in the light of a doubtful and dangerous financial experiment, except the builders were saddled with the restriction that in all their purchases of iron and steel they should be obliged to take, irrespective of kind or quality, such products as the American iron and steel manufacturers might offer to sell, and none other. Now it might naturally have been supposed, in conformity with the old proverb, "What is sauce for the goose is sauce for the gander," that the American iron and steel manufactories, having prohibited the transcontinental railroad companies from using any thing but American iron and steel for their constructions, would have themselves rigidly refrained from using anything in turn in their iron and steel works, except the products of American labor. But if any one had indulged in such an hypothesis he would have been sadly disappointed. For these special iron and steel friends of American industry no sooner found out that in the absence of a hundred per cent. duty on foreign pig iron, scrap-iron and iron-ore, they could supply themselves with these raw materials cheaper in the foreign than in the domestic market, than they deliberately turned their backs on their fellow-American iron miners and pig-metal smelters, and proceeded to take advantage of the pauper labor of Europe by purchasing and importing large quantities of iron ore from Spain, and old rails and scrap iron from England and other countries, the importation of foreign ore for 1880 having amounted to 493,408 tons ; and old rail and scrap to the value of $14,705,879. Whereat much harsh language and not a few threats of smashing the protective machine have been indulged in on the part of American workingmen, who have always been told by the protectionists of the Pennsylvania school that good Americans must only buy and manufacture American products, and never omit to frown down severely the products of the pauper labor of Europe. Another result of this absurd legislation has been to put at least one of the Pacific railroads in a very awkward position. This is the act of Congress incorporating the Texas & Pacific railroad, passed March 3. 1871. It was provided (Section 16.) at the instance of Pennsylvania iron and steel manufacturers, "that said road should be constructed of iron or steel rails manufactured exclusively from American ores, except such as may heretofore have been contracted for by any railroad company which may be purchased or consolidated with by being qualified and incorporated as provided in this act." and a supplementary act. approved March 2. 1872, repeats almost the same language. Now as none of the Bessemer steel rail mills in Pennsylvania use American ores and iron exclusively and solely, but all import large quantities of foreign ores from Spain, Elba, and other foreign mines ; and as probably no company in the whole country is able to dispense with the use of so-called "speigel eisen," (a foreign manganese iron) : it follows that if the strict letter and intent of the law was carried out, the Texas & Pacific railroad would be actually debarred from purchasing a single steel rail, under any existing circumstances in any market.

Let us still turn another leaf in this curious history of the American Bessemer Steel Monopoly. Heretofore it has been found impracticable to make Bessemer steel of iron produced from ores containing sulphur or phosphorus in appreciable quantities, and as most English and Americaan ores of iron contain these substances, the supply of proper iron has been a somewhat expensive and troublesome matter to both English and American Bessemer steel makers. Within a very recent period, however, a method known as the "Gilchrest-Thomas process," has been discovered in England, whereby at small expense any ore of iron can be used for the manufacture of Bessemer steel; and the patent right to its exclusive use in the United States has been also purchased by the American Bessemer Steel Association. According to the last report of the American Iron and Steel Association (July, 1881), this new process "has been successfully adopted in nearly all the steel making countries of Europe," and "that England thus adds another to the list of her important inventions effecting the manufacture of iron and steel." But the United States alone of all the steel making countries in the world, has not yet adopted this great improvement; and apparently will not for the present. For it is well understood that the "eleven associates" who own the patents for the "Thomas-Gilchrest process" in the United States, do not find it for their interest, with the present ratio of profits on the manufacture of Bessemer steel, to adopt any innovations; and that they further do not propose to issue licenses to anybody else to use it, for any royalty which it would be possible to pay. And thus in the name of protection to American industry, the march of improvement and the cheapening of a great necessity of civilization are arrested.

We read in history of examples of European monarchs granting to court favorites and kept mistresses exclusive right to deal in salt, gold lace, glass, leather, and other commodities, with a view of enriching the recipients and owners of these privileges by taxing the consumption of the people. And in all these cases the tax was purposely made indirect so that the amount of the robbery should not be readily comprehended and appreciated by the sufferers. Most people suppose that the day for all this sort of imposition has long gone by : but it would be difficult to find in all history a single instance of so monstrous abuse of the rights of the people to buy, sell and use freely, as is embodied and practiced under the claim of benefiting domestic industry, by the American Bessemer Steel Monopoly.

In the Arabian Nights it was necessary to tell a thousand and one stories before the Sultan of the Indies could be persuaded of the impropriety of cutting off a wife's head every morning before breakfast. The American people have been so long imposed upon in respect to the workings of the existing tariff and so assiduously taught to believe that a continuation of these impositions is essential to the continuance of national prosperity, that possibly they will require a thousand and one further illustrations of the iniquity of the Pennsylvanian system of protection, before they be convinced of its impolicy and wickedness and reform it out of existence. But, be this as it may, one would think that sufficient evidence has been submitted to satisfy the public that some important measures of tariff reform ought to be immediately instituted, and that it is not necessary to have a tariff commission to find out how and where to begin.

[*Extract from "Bradstreet's," Jan. 16th, 1886.*]

SUGAR AND THE TARIFF.

Probably no other article upon our extensive list of dutiable staples presents such anomalies as that of sugar. With the exception of, say, ten or fifteen years, when the country had to raise its revenue through every practicable source, the tariff upon sugar has been entirely a protective one. It has been framed, particularly during the past twenty years, with special care and with a view to develope the production of domestic sugar. It also happens that a small portion of the country under favorable influences is suited to the production of cane sugar. Considering that the object of the present tariff is purely the developement of American industry, it is only natural to expect that an article which is protected to the extent of about 60 per cent. should show a marvelous growth, particularly so when that article is one of the most popular kind, and to a large extent necessary to the full enjoyment of life, for sugar can no longer be ranked as a luxury. If, however, the production of domestic sugar is statistically considered, it will be found that the production has not increased under a most patronizing tariff, but absolutely decreased.

	Hhd.		Hhd		Hhd.		Hhd.
1823	30,000	1839	115,000	1855	231,427	1870	144,881
1824	32,000	1840	87,000	1856	73,296	1871	128,461
1825	36,000	1841	90,000	1857	279,697	1872	108,520
1826	45,000	1842	140,000	1858	362,269	1873	89,498
1827	71,000	1843	100,000	1859	221,840	1874	116,867
1828	88,000	1844	200,000	1860	228,753	1875	144,146
1829	48,000	1845	186,000	1861	459,419	1876	169,331
1830	no data	1846	140,000	1862	no data	1877	127,753
1831	no data	1847	240,000	1863	76,800	1878	213,221
1832	70,000	1848	226,000	1864	10,387	1879	169,972
1833	75,000	1849	247,923	1865	18,070	1880	218,314
1834	100,000	1850	211,201	1866	41,000	1881	122,982
1835	30,000	1851	237,547	1867	37,647	1882	241,220
1836	70,000	1852	321,934	1868	84,256	1883	221,515
1837	65,000	1853	449,324	1869	87,090	1884	170,431
1838	70,000	1854	346,635				

The above table gives the production of cane sugar as far back as reliable data can be obtained. The figures given are hogsheads.

The table presents quite a study to all revenue reformers. With one single exception 1853 was the most productive year in the list, and at that time, strange to say, the duty averaged only .95c. per pound, against 1.95c. for 1884. If, however, we take 1867, when the duty upon all imported sugar averaged 3.04c., which is within .02 of the bond price for the past year, it will be seen that the production only amounted to 37.647 hogsheads. Granted that the war wrought considerable havoc in the sugar producing regions, but it was over and there was a time for a revival. The same rate of duty continued until 1870 but with little better results, the crop only amounting to 144,881 hogsheads. If, however, a further comparison is made of 1881, which is eleven years later, and when the duty averaged 2.46c. per pound, it will be seen that the production instead of increasing at an enormous rate, as might be expected, it absolutely declined to 122.982 hogsheads, or a decrease of over 15 per cent. in eleven years. This decrease was during the time when the lowest tariff averaged for the year over 2c. per pound. Further, if the crop of 1884 be compared with that of 1853 the comparison will be still against a continuance of an excessive tariff for the development of an industry that resists 60 per cent. protection. In 1853 the production, as stated before, amounted to 449,324 hogsheads, while last year's production reached but 170,431 hogsheads or 277,893 hogsheads less. We therefore produced over 160 per cent. more sugar in 1853 with a tariff of .95c. per pound than we did with a tariff of 1.95c. in 1884. The difference in the price of sugar is only slightly against 1884, the average price of fair refining being, for the latter year 3.31c. against 3.49c. in 1853, a difference of only 18c. If, however, 1869 is taken, the comparison, so far as price is concerned, becomes much more favorable to the domestic product. The production in that year was about 87,090 hogsheads, which is a reduction of 362.234 hogsheads, while the average price in bond was 5.56c. against 3.49c. respectively, or 2.07c. in

favor of 1869. In the light of statistics, viewed from the point
of production alone, our domestic sugar production is un-
questionably a complete failure, the figures given above
proving beyond dispute that the industry flourished better
under a low than a high tariff. It may be argued by the
friends of the sugar producer that the conditions of labor have
changed, and owing to the abolition of slavery it is more difficult to compete with the imported article, even if the duty is
60 per cent. It must not be forgotten, however, that slavery
has been abolished in nearly every other sugar producing
country, and that in many of them labor is quite as high as it
is in the Southern States.

It is urged that the cost of production, caused by the difference in the price of labor, prevents our Southern planters from
competing with foreign-grown sugar. This, however, is only
partially true, for in many countries sugar is grown with labor
equally as dear as that in any cane-sugar producing State. It
is safe to say that in most countries where labor is free the cost
is equal to labor in the South.

It is not the labor cost that is the greatest item in sugar production, although it is an important one, and in order that a
fair comparison may be made upon this point, the following
table, which is authentic, will show that in the Hawaiian
Islands the skilled labor is higher than in Louisiana. The un-
skilled laborer is allowed to work but ten hours a day in the
mill, and twelve in the field :

OCCUPATION.	NO. EMPLOYED.	COST PER DAY.
Firemen,	3 men	$3 00
Water tender,	1 man	1 00
Putting cane in carrier,	10 men	10 00
Feeding mill,	2 men	2 00
Backing megass,	1 man	1 00
Taking megass to house,	3 men	3 00
Taking megass from house to boilers,	7 men	7 00
At juice pump strainer,	1 boy	50
Assisting engineer,	1 man	1 00
At clarifiers,	2 men	2 00
At cleaners,	2 men	2 00

Amount carried forward $32 50

Amount brought forward,		$32 50
At double effect,	1 man	1 50
At filter press,	2 men, 1 boy	2 50
At centrifugals,	2 men	2 00
At coolers,	2 men	2 00
Packing sugar,	2 men	2 00
Sewing bags,	1 woman	50
Sugar clerk,	1 man	2 00
Watchman,	1 man	1 00
Total,		$46 00

Average day's work 21,000 gallons juice, equal to
18 tons sugar; cost per ton for unkilled labor: 2 55
Skilled labor per year, or crop:

Engineer,	$1,800
Sugar boiler,	1,500
Total,	$3,300

For a crop of say 3,000 tons (2,000 pounds each),
per ton, 1 10

Total cost of labor, per ton, $3 65

The advantage with the sugar planter on the Hawaiian Islands is the superiority of machinery, this machinery being more easily obtained because it is imported free of duty. In this respect our Southern planter is placed at a disadvantage.

The labor problem is not the difficulty with the Southern planter. It is lack of capital, and the inadaptability of the climate which are the greatest drawbacks to the profitable production of sugar in this country. If these are facts, and they are admitted by all who have any intimate knowledge of planting, then why support an industry by exorbitant duties which can never supply more than an average of 12 per cent. of the consumptive demand? Those planters who have plenty of capital, and there are a few who have, with modern machinery, could produce sugar at a profit at present prices, with a duty of not more than 25 per cent. But to keep up a tariff of 60 per cent. in order to keep alive those who labor under insurmountable difficulties, is neither just to the consumers of sugar, nor is it a wise or statesmanlike policy to pursue.

If, however, the present tariff on sugar is examined broadly, its exorbitance becomes much more distinct. The following table gives the amount of sugar imported in the fiscal year ending June 30. 1884. which is a representative year.

Foreign sugar 2.562.719.593 pounds net.	$103,884,760
Duty on same.	47.500.749
Domestic sugar. all kinds,	43.922,169
	$195.307,678

To this amount must be added the cost of refining, handling, etc.. which would bring up the amount to considerably over $200.000.000 per annum. even if the exports are deducted. This would give a net cost per capita of about $4. Thus, if the per capita consumption of wheat is taken at 5 bushels, the national sugar bill equals that of wheat. When it is considered that this sugar bill, through the operation of the present tariff, is unnecessarily increased over $70.000.000 annually, with a view to maintain a languishing industry. it appears somewhat strange that tariff reformers are so very reticent upon this question. In no other article does the tariff tax weigh upon the workman so severely as that of sugar. At the present moment the north-western wheat producer is compelled to sell his wheat in an open market and against labor and a climate that is entirely against him. yet he is obliged to pay more than treble as much for his sugar as his competitor. Take the English farmer: he can purchase his sugar at three and one-half cents per pound, while in the north-west our farmer has to pay from seven and one-half cents to eight cents for exactly the same quality. If, however, we compare the India wheat producer, the comparison is much more unfavorable. India produces sugar at less cost than any other country in the world. and the quality of sugar used by the Indian wheat producer, while being inferior to that consumed by the American farmer, does not cost at the outside more than 2c. per pound. or about one fourth the cost of sugar to our wheat producer. In the face of such facts how is it possible for our farmer to compete with Indian wheat? By our present tariff taxes the wheat producer and the sugar consumer pay over $70.000.000 a year in order to protect our sugar industry.

If it were possible to ever produce sufficient sugar to meet our consumptive requirements at a reasonable cost there would be at least some reason for maintaining the present tariff. But there is not. If we cannot produce sugar at less than 60 per cent. more than other countries. why waste our land on fruitless attempts to build up an artificial industry. The bulk of this $70.000.000 is paid by the industrial and producing class of the country. Thus we handicap ourselves to this extent by taxing such a necessary of life as sugar. Free sugar would reduce the cost to the consumers on the Pacific coast fully one half, or, in other words, it would put about $3.500.000 into their pockets annually. Our statesmen will do well to ask the question why it is that sugar should have such a large share in producing revenue. and upon what grounds this excessive tax is continued? It cannot be supported from a necessitous point as our revenue is ample. As a protective experiment it has utterly failed. for the industry has declined during the past forty years. Not more than 12 per cent. of our consumptive requirements can be produced under the most favorable circumstances. and to produce this the consumer is made to pay over $70,000,000 more than the absolute value of the product. Under such conditions the tariff upon sugar demands revision at least. No industry extending over half a century as sugar has should require such an expenditure to keep alive. particularly when it weighs so heavily upon the poorer portion of our population. There are abundant reasons therefore. which demand that the attention of our legislators should be directed towards a more equal and just tariff on sugar.

AMERICAN SHIPPING.

MY DEAR MR. KELLY.

Your note has been received. I seldom meddle with statistics. Figures can be made to lie as well as to tell the truth. The arguments for free trade are not based upon arithmetic. They have the solid foundation of justice, liberty, and the inalienable right of men to control their own property for their own benefit, and not for that of others. However, I think I may for once make use of figures in answering your question regarding the rise and fall of American Commercial Shipping from 1840 to 1886.

In 1840 our tonnage engaged in foreign trade was 762.838 tons. In 1885 it was 1,262.814 tons. It had increased from 1840 to 1861, so that in that year it amounted to 2,496.894 tons. From that date its downward career commenced and lessened with increasing ratio until as just stated in 1885, it was just about one-half of what it was at its highest point.

I thank you for asking the questions because in my search I find a singular accompaniment of this rise and fall. In 1840 the average duty on imports was 34.39 per cent. In 1861, when our tonnage was at its height the average duty was only 18.84 per cent., and in 1885, while the tonnage is sliding downwards, the average duty 46.07 per cent. is higher than any that has existed since the year 1831. There is something very significant about these figures. It seems to me that they may account for some part of the decline of our shipping. Ask some of your protectionist friends.

Perhaps they can explain them by making them lie, for that is the only way in which the thing can be done. After they have satisfied themselves on this point with the old explanation that our commercial marine came to grief because of the civil war, ask them these few questions from the marine catechism :

Was not the matter brought to the attention of the public before the civil war, and before the misfortune forseen commenced?

Was there any decline while the business of the ocean was carried on in wooden sailing ships. Did anybody ask for bounty then?

Was not the cost of wooden sailing ships as low or perhaps lower in the United States than in England?

During the civil war was not the transition going on from the wooden sailing ship to the iron screw steamship?

When we came out of the war did we not find ourselves virtually without either?

Were we very sory to get rid of our useless old sailing ships?

Were we not sorry that we could not replace them with iron steamships?

Were not our captains, officers, and sailors then out of employment because of this impossibility?

Who are protected by our system of protection. Shipbuilders who build no ships or foreigners who are doing our carrying trade because our own people are not allowed to participate in it?

I believe I have answered the questions you proposed to me. Now call on the protectionists to stand up. They will find it easier to tackle the Assembly's Catechism than to wrestle with this.

Yours very truly,

John Codman.

D. D. Kelly, Esq.

FREE TRADE.

BY THE RT. HON. W. E. GLADSTONE.

A speech delivered at Leeds, England, October, 1881.

Mr. Gladstone said : Mr. Kitson and Gentlemen.—I am very sensible of the great honor which you have done me to-day in presenting me with this address. It contains, in short compass, allusions to many points of the greatest importance. So far as those embrace the legislative action of the Government, I need not, I think, assure you of our great anxiety to make progress in the direction, and generally in the manner that you desire : but it is only right that I should call your attention—and, indeed I must take every opportunity that presents itself of calling the attention of the public at large—to the very serious obstacles that now impede the progress of business in the House of Commons, and to assure you that for the sake of every interest, and for the sake of every measure, it has become a matter of vital importance to consider in what way that great and noble legislative instrument, the House of Commons—itself the noblest legislative instrument in the world—can be restored to that efficiency which it once possessed, if possible even with an extension and increase of that efficiency. Because, gentlemen, experience has proved that with the progress of time and with the great accumulation of legislative labors of which this century has been the witness, instead of clearing off the call upon us for fresh exertion, the developing wants of an enlarged society continually augment the long catalogue of our arrears, and if we are to deal with them seriously it must be not only by approaching each of them with the instrumental power we now possess, but by attempting some great and effectual improvement in the rules for working the instrument itself.

There is, however, one of these questions to which I will particularly refer—the question of the French Treaty now under negotiation—though adjourned negotiation, still under negotiation—with the Commissioners in France. I will not anticipate the results of that negotiation. It would be premature. But as to the basis on which the negotiation is conducted you may rely upon it that we are in no doubt or difficulty. We think that we understand the general sentiment of the British public—the commercial public—upon the subject, and our own opinions are in conformity with that sentiment. I, for my part, look back with the deepest interest upon the share that I had in concluding—at least I will not say so much in concluding—but in conducting on this side of the water, and within the walls of Parliament as well as in administration, the proceedings which led to that memorable French treaty in 1860. It is quite true that that treaty did not produce the whole of the effects that some too sanguine anticipations may possibly have expected from it—that it did not produce a universal smash of protective duties as I wish it had throughout the civilized world. But it did something. It enormously increased the trade between this country and France. It knit more closely than they had ever been knit before the sentiments of good will between this country and France. It effectually checked and traversed in the year 1860 tendencies of a very different kind towards needless alarms and panics and tendencies towards convulsion and confusion in Europe. There was no more powerful instrument for confining and controling those wayward and angry spirits, at that particular crisis, than the commercial treaty with France. It produced no inconsiderable effect for a number of years upon the legislation of various European countries, which tended less decisively than we could have desired, but still intelligibly and beneficially, in the direction of freedom of trade.

There has been of late a reaction, as we know, in various countries. The political economy of Germany walks in a direction adverse to ours. But as I have said, and I do not hesitate to repeat it to you, when we observe what notions are abroad in our country, what doctrines are held, what specifics are recommended for the purpose of recovering trade from its partial contraction—I won't say decay, for decayed it has not—but from its partial contraction. I think we cannot very much wonder if the same errors have scope and go abroad in other countries and have more influence on the legislation of other countries than, after our large and rich experience, they are likely to have in ours. For although, as this is not a political assembly, I have not the slightest intention to make a political speech to you, yet I may say that I express the firmest and strongest conviction that no Government that can exist in this country will either soon or late pledge its responsibility to any proposals for restoring protective duties. You might as well attempt to overthrow any institution of the country as to over-throw the Free Trade legislation. It is not in vain that a country of this kind, with the opportunities that, thank God, we possess for free deliberation, devotes a quarter of a century of its life towards breaking down its ancient and complicated tariff and making its trade free to all the world. We are not in the habit of undoing our great legislative acts. Foreign observers of the proceedings of this country find much to criti-cise, fin I something to admire, and one of the subjects which they select for admiration is this, that progress in this country, if it be not always rapid, yet is always sure, and that when we have made steps in advance we do not follow them by undoing our own labor and making steps in retreat. And therefore, gentlemen, as regards this legislation, you might as well at-tempt to overthrow trial by jury; you might as well attempt to overthrow the right of petition or of public meeting; you might as well attempt to tear out of our social and political system, any one of the most cherished ideas that Englishmen have inherited from centuries of history, as to overset the Free Trade legislation. Do not suppose that on that account it is my opinion that the strange theories that have now for a moment lifted their heads from their native obscurity into light are matters of small importance, or will do no mischief.

I have spoken on this subject in another place. They may become the subject matter of very serious conflict between parties; they may create and propagate delusion in various quarters and places of the country; they may be made use of for this or that particular view; they may influence this or that election; they may lead to great waste of time, and to a good deal of confusion in the relations of party and politics—all these are evils which I hope we shall be able to obviate and to keep down. But I wish to point out to you that at least, in my firm conviction, there is a limit to these evils, and that the great legislation which marked the lifetime of Sir Robert Peel, of Mr. Cobden, and with which the name of Mr. Bright is inseparably connected—is, in my opinion, resting upon such foundations that nothing can shake it, and that the speeches and the articles, and the treaties that are now floating about in the atmosphere pass as the wind around the solid structure within whose walls we stand, and have no more effect than the idle breeze has upon the stones of this solid structure.

I ought to say one word more before I pass from this subject. I must say a word upon the subject of the Commercial Treaty with France. I read with great interest the remarks of Sir Stafford Northcote on this subject, and I am bound to say that I think they state the case very fairly. It is a balance of the considerations which we had to take into view. There are great disadvantages attaching to all commercial treaties, and the most serious disadvantage of them all is this, that there is a great tendency—when you are only suggesting to people that they should do what is good for themselves—there is a great tendency to assume the position of requesting them to do something simply because it is good for you. There is a tendency to misrepresent and dislocate, if I may say so, the true idea of commerce, which rests and is founded upon this principle—that in the operations of commerce it is absolutely impossible for a country to do good to itself without at the same time doing good to other people. You may depend upon this, gentlemen—I cannot undertake at this moment to say, though we have good hopes—I will not undertake at this moment to say whether we shall have a treaty with France or not; but upon this you may rely, that much as we value association with France, great as is the political value of a well concluded commercial negotiation, we do not think it our duty, nor within the limits of our rights to purchase that political advantage by a sacrifice of the true principles of our commercial relations; and if you have a treaty with France, you may depend upon it that it shall not be, with our assent, taking it all in all, a treaty of retrogression either small or great.

I will not say many words to you about myself. Although I spring from a commercial family, yet when I entered Parliament it was not for a good many years that my mind was turned to economical subjects; in truth, it was not until 1841, when, on the proposal of Sir Robert Peel, I accepted the office of Vice-President of the Board of Trade. At that period the Board of Trade was the department which administered to a great extent the functions, which have since then passed principally into the hands of the Treasury, connected with the fiscal laws of the country. I had inherited, as nearly the whole Conservative party had, and likewise, as you know, no inconsiderable portion of the Liberal party down to that period had inherited the ideas and traditions of Protection. But when it became my duty in the Board of trade to apply myself, with the energies of youth which I then possessed, to the consideration of those subjects, I need not say that I found those traditions crumble away rapidly under my feet, and before I had been there twelve months my name had become a by-word, and was quoted in Protectionist assemblies as that of a man who was not to be trusted. It was quite true, gentlemen. Moreover, they found out about the same time that Sir Robert Peel could not be trusted, and not only that, but as we got older and older, and lived on from year to year, the matter got worse and worse, and we became still less worthy of the public confidence on the ground of maintaining any system of Protection. Well, now, gentlemen, as we are in an assembly of no vast numbers, although of great influence and power, and as we are not met upon political or party grounds, let me call your attention for a few minutes to a subject which I purposely omitted yesterday in my address in a larger room. The main proposition is capable of being considered with the utmost calmness and coolness—whether we have been right, after all,

in what we have been doing, or whether a great delusion has
passed upon us. And I do this, not for your sakes, or for my
own, but for the sake of weaker brethren—if I may so venture
to call them—who really have, in certain cases and in various
classes of the community, embraced, and I have no doubt in
perfect good faith, the belief that we have been acting under a
delusion, and that Free Trade has been an error and a failure.
Fortunately it does not require to be discussed at any great
length, and I think I can go through it without making any
outrageous claim upon your patience.

I take the date of 1840 as that of the last year in which the
protective system enjoyed perfect peace. In every year after
that it was subject to a series of discussions and disturbances,
which, in the first place, produced the most grievous effects
upon its health; and, in the second led to its utter downfall.
But before 1840 what was the condition of the country? If I
regard the condition of this country as to wealth, I find that
between the beginning of the century and 1840 there was a
very large increase of the population, owing to causes partly
healthful and partly otherwise, but the wealth of the country
increased in a less proportion than the population; and what
was much more important was this, it increased in the hands
of the class already possessed of wealth, but no share of this increase went to the mass of the people. I am afraid I am correct in saying, that if we take the mass of our agricultural
population in particular, the history of these years was a
history of going from bad to worse, a history of increasing
social degradation, a history of absolute want in various degrees, and in many or most of the counties in this country, of
the means of decent lodging, decent clothing, and sufficient
feeding, until that great Act, one of the wisest and most important of modern legislation, the new Poor Law Act, was
passed in 1834, and with slow and sure operation began to
check the more grievous forms of certain mischiefs, but of
course without the power of being able to supply the new vital
energies which had to be sought in other quarters. That,
generally speaking, was our material condition. And what
was our moral condition? I well remember, on the first

occasion of my entering Parliament how we heard from well-intentioned men the sorest and the most just lamentations over the increase of crime under the blessed influence of Protection, and a well-informed author quotes the numbers thus for the crimes committed in England and taken notice of by public justice: that in 1809 they had been 5,350; in 1818 they had swollen, after the Peace, and with the special causes of distress that the Peace and that the unhappy Corn Law brought with them, they had swollen to 14,254; and in 1829 they rose to 18,675. That, gentlemen, I give you as an indication of the moral influences attaching to the system of Protection, because I warn and entreat you never to be content to argue the question of free commerce as if it were a material question alone. It is just as strong in its political, in its social, and in its moral aspects as it is in its operation upon the production and increase of wealth.

That is all I will say to you on the state of things before 1840. Now, let me consider what has happened since 1840. In 1841, the population of this country—the three kingdoms—was twenty-six and a-half millions. In 1881 the population had increased to 35 millions; the increase was eight and a-half millions, or very nearly, and closely enough for my present purpose, an increase of 33 per cent. Now, I want to compare, first with the increased population the increase of wealth, and though I shall resort to the Income-tax in the first place for this purpose, I shall do it safely, because we all know that, while the wealthy classes have been growing wealthier, the poorer classes have likewise been gradually emerging from their indigence, and that freedom of commerce has showered its benefits over them, speaking generally, with no less liberality and no less efficiency than over the capitalists of this country. The increase of wages in this country has borne, if not a full proportion, yet some proportion to the increase of capital, and has formed a solid addition to the comforts of the people, such as, at any rate, whether sufficient or not—and of that I need not speak—is without example in our prior history. Let me look at the progress of wealth as shown by the Income-tax. The income taxable to the Income-tax in 1842 was

251 millions; in 1880 it was 542 millions. I don't include Ireland in the return. Very large amounts of income had in the meantime, whether wisely or unwisely—and I need not enter on that subject now—been either wholly or partially excluded, and I think that the tax may have lost as much as 40 millions of taxable income in that way. That would make £582.000.000 to compare with £251.000. The result of that is, that while the population of the country had grown 33 per cent. the wealth of the country, instead of growing as it had done before at a rate slower than the population, had increased, and, tested by the Income-tax, at the rate of 130 per cent; and if we were able to exhibit the mass of the income of labor, it is probable that it would have exhibited a growth hardly, if at all less remarkable. The trade of the country increased by the exports of British produce; and in this increase of exports I need not say the working people have a share perhaps as important even as the capitalist. Where in 1840 they were £51.000.000. in 1880 they were £223,000,000; so that while the population of the country had grown 33 per cent., the export trade of the country had grown at the rate of 340 per cent. As to the savings of the mass of the population—I only quote this as a partial fact of interest, for we have unfortunately no effectual means of exhibiting the subject completely—the savings deposited in savings banks, which had been £24.500.000 in 1840 were £75.500.000 in 1880; and undoubtedly that £75.500.000 was far more representative of the savings of the working classes through the Post Office savings banks in 1880 than the £24.500.000 in 1840 had been representative of the savings of that class.

If I turn to the other side, what was the condition of the country in regard to pauperism and crime? The earliest returns that I have found of the able-bodied paupers of England and Wales gives for 1849 a number of 201.000; and for 1880. with a vastly larger population, a number of 111.000. Still more important than the returns of pauperism is the return of crime, and the persons convicted of crime, who in 1840 had risen to 34.000; in 1881, according to our returns, which may not precisely exhibit the proper state of things—because

changes have taken place as between summary and non-sum-
mary jurisdiction, but which, upon the whole, will exhibit
them—these convictions had sunk from 34,000 to 15,600. I
have kept my word in so far that these facts have been presented to you in a brief and summary form. But are they not
administrative and conclusive facts? Is it possible for any
reasonable man not to be satisfied with figures like these?

As to the reality of our progress, and as to the cause of our
progress, I will say another word shortly. Still there are de-
lusions—at least there are uncomfortable dreams to break the
rest of some of our fellow citizens. They are dreadfully
afflicted with this excess of imports. In passing I must pay a
tribute of respect to one class of Protectionists, and that is to
the gallant men who, under all circumstances, with following
or without following, with proof or without proof, and quite
irrespective of the possibility of being able to turn the matter
to account at elections, stick to their old protective doctrine.
I mention that because the subject of the balance of trade irre-
sistibly and rapidly calls to my mind the name and figure of
Mr. Newdegate, who has been a consistent, but I must say a
highly respectable prophet of evil, and respected for his un-
swerving integrity, and for the great regard he has often shown
for Constitutional principles in connection with this painful
subject of the balance of trade. But you are aware by the old
doctrine of the balance of trade it is shown we have suffered a
loss of 160 millions of money within a comparatively short
period—about a generation of man. This is a very heavy loss
and how have we paid for it? Oh, you pay for all that in bullion. Well, but the extraordinary fact is this. Here the
balance of trade has been most terribly against us during the
last five years. From 1876 to 1880, when the imports—these
terrible imports that frown upon us and intimidate us in every
port of the country as if they were all meant for dynamite ex-
plosions—these imports have been in an excess of £622,000,000
over the exports, and yet the country is not absolutely ruined.
But while these £622,000,000 have been imported—and we
have certainly had to pay for what we have imported—
instead of losing the bullion, the imports of bullion have been

slightly in excess of the exports. The imports of bullion for these five years have amounted to £147.000.000, and the exports have amounted to £144.000.000, so that besides the £622,000.000 of goods which we have got, we have got £3.000.000 more bullion into the country. But, then it is said, "Oh, but we have paid for it in securities." Why, sir, anyone who goes into the money market will know that the investments of England abroad, varying somewhat from year to year, have been tending rapidly and constantly upwards; and were we here to examine into and analyze the history and meaning of these vast imports, you know very well it would be my duty to point out that no inconsiderable proportion of them represents the dividends and the interest receivable and received by us upon our enormous investments abroad—investments which are valued by the best financial authorities—non-official, but the best private authorities—at about 1.300 millions of money, and the income from which, coming back to us every year, mainly in the shape of imports, cannot be said to be less than 60 millions a year—our income in foreign countries from the surplus of wealth which we have sent out of our country to invest.

So much, gentlemen, for the balance of trade. But still they are not satisfied; and you are taught to believe that the foreign trade of this country is wasting away, and that other countries, owing to their greater wisdom, have none of the inconveniences to contend with that we are obliged to encounter, and are constantly growing in all the elements of prosperity. And the two countries which our misguided brethren select for special admiration are America and France. Well, now, the commerce of France, above all others, requires to be divided when you treat its exports between manufactures and produce, because the exports of its produce go on without any material reference to this protective system. Our exports, as you know very well, fell seriously between 1873 and 1879. But do you suppose—because we are invited to assume—that the exports of manufactured goods in other countries did not similarly fall? How did France, with its protective system, fare in respect to the decrease of exports? Our exports fell from a high degree to one comparatively much reduced, but not so much reduced as the exports of French manufactures, for the manufactures exported by France in 1849 were £49,000.000 sterling ; in 1879 they had sunk to £34.000.000 sterling, and that was a greater diminution measured by per centage than the diminution which took place in this country. So that the existence of the protective system did not in the slightest degree mitigate, but on the contrary, aggravated a decline in the export of manufactured goods, as it would do in this country, if, unhappily, we were to be so unwise—which we never shall be—as to try this deadly experiment.

Well, now, there is also an idea that America is pursuing a course of profound wisdom in regard to its protective system, and we are told that under the blessed shelter of a system of that kind the tender infancy of trades is cherished, which afterwards, having obtained vigor, will go forth into neutral markets and possess the world. Gentlemen, is that true? America has been too long in various degrees a protective country. Have the manufacturers of America gone forth and possessed the world? How do they compete with you in those quarters of the world which are, speaking generally, outside the influences of Protection? Gentlemen, to the whole of Asia, to the whole of Africa, and to the whole of Australasia—which in the main, are outside this question, and may fairly be described in the rough as presenting to us neutral markets, where we meet America without fear or favor, one way or the other—the whole of the exports of the United States of manufactured goods to those countries amount to £4,751.000 ; while the exports to those same quarters from the United Kingdom were £78,140.000. Gentlemen, the fact is this—America is a young country, with enormous vigor and enormous internal resources. She has committed—I say it, I hope, not with disrespect : I say it with strong and cordial sympathy, but with much regret—she is committing errors of which we set her an example. But from the enormous resources of her home market, the development of which internally is not touched by Protection, she is able to commit those errors with less fatal consequences, with less inconvenient consequences upon her people than we experienced when we committed them; and the enormous development of American resources within, casts almost entirely into the shade the puny character of the export of her manufactures to the neutral markets of the world. And here, gentlemen, I am reminded that I was guilty on a certain occasion of stating in an article—not a political article—that, in my opinion, it was far from improbable that as the volume of the future was unrolled, America, with its vast population and its wonderful resources, and not less with that severe education which, from the high price of labor, America is receiving in the strong necessity of resorting to every description of labor-saving contrivances, and the consequent development, not only on a large scale, but down to the smallest scale of the mechanical genius of the country—on that account, the day may come when that country may claim to possess the commercial primacy of the world. I gave sad offence to many—to many of those who tell you that they are ruined already. They were extremely annoyed and offended on account of this, which was not a positive prediction, but an intimation of a probability. I won't enter into it now. I know that was an offence to the vanity of those who are vain among us. But for my part, gentlemen, I think it one of the most sacred duties of a public man to tell the things which he thinks to be of interest and importance, and which may perhaps convey a salutary warning to his countrymen, whether his countrymen like to hear them or not; and I will say this, that as long as America adheres to the Protective system, your commercial primacy is secure. Nothing in the world can wrest it from you while America continues to fetter her own strong hands and arms, and with these fettered arms is content to compete with you, who are free, in neutral markets. And as long as America follows the doctrine of Protection, or as long as America follows the doctrines now known as those of Fair Trade, you are perfectly safe, and you need not allow, any of you, even your lightest slumbers to be disturbed by the fear that America will take from you your commercial primacy.

Now, gentlemen, let us see what is our case with regard to the trade of the world. We in this country—whose life-blood the vampire of Free Trade is insidiously sucking—let us see what share in this little island we have got of the Free Trade of the world. In 1880 our trade with the world amounted to 698 millions in value, the largest, I believe, ever known of imports and exports taken together, and, of course, re-exports as well. In 1873, the year of our largest exports, I believe the total trade represented 682 millions. But I will take our worst year—the year 1879, which was the year the darkness of which called forth all the owls and the bats of the country and sent them croaking abroad in order to disturb us, and if possible to teach us to walk in the ways of another policy—in 1879, it is quite true, the trifling sum of 612 millions was all that passed through our hands in this business of exchange, with a population of 35 millions of people. Well, now, let us compare the trade and population of some other countries. The German Empire, with 40 millions of people, had 371 millions of trade. The United States, with 50 millions of people, had 239 millions of external trade, most of which, or an enormous share of which, you know was owing to our demand for the food and provisions that, thank God, she produces. And while we, with a population of 35 millions, had a trade of 612 millions, these two countries together—two of the most civilized countries in the world, both of them highly protective—had with a population of 90 millions, a trade of 610 millions; so that comparing ourselves with these great and intelligent countries, man with man, you have nearly three times the amount of trade there is in their hands. Take, again, three other countries which I take on account of the large figures they present, their high place in the trade of the world. France has 313 millions of trade, with 36 millions of people. Russia has 183 millions of trade, with 80 millions of people. Holland has 116 millions of trade—a good deal of which, as we all know, is transit trade for the supply of the interior parts of the Continent—Holland, I say, has 116 millions of trade, with five millions, say of people. Then again, we have a population of 121 millions, with a trade of 612 millions, exactly that which in the disastrous year of 1879 fell to our share with a people of 35 millions.

Now the reason I have quoted these particulars is because I have not yet encountered that which is the favorite plea of our erring brethren—namely, that this is all owing to the railways and the telegraphs. You know that is what they say. They say, "We admit there is some increase in trade." They do admit positively that 450 millions is a larger sum than 51 millions—but it is all owing to the railways and telegraphs; but if it is owing to the railways and telegraphs, why have not the railways and telegraphs carried the trade of the world from our hands to the hands of Germany, America, France, Russia and Holland, which are full of railways and telegraphs—some of them even fuller than we are? Why are they not pointing to our depression of trade and showing how small our population and trade are—for they are protective countries except Holland—showing how small they are in comparison with theirs, instead of pointing to them in irrefragible figures showing that Free Trade *plus* the railways have done for us ten times more than Protection *plus* railways have done for France, or America, or for Germany, or for any of the rest of the countries.

And, gentlemen, that brings me to the last point that I intend to argue, but, really, I have made very little argument. I have not required to make argument, or to wander into the mazes of political economy. Very simple facts and figures, after all not outrageous in their number, have constituted the pith and the substance of the statement I have laid before you. But I am desirous if I can to get rid of this remaining false impression about the railways and the telegraphs, which have done an infinity of good for us; but at the same time I am perhaps entitled to say—because through the medium of one of our most widely circulating monthly magazines, before the cares of office were upon me, I endeavored to make a very close and careful analysis by comparison of the consequences of railway and telegraphic enterprise on the one side and of commercial legislation in the direction of freedom on the other, and seemed to myself to establish—at any rate no one has contested the argument—the conclusion that, although very much is due to the railways and telegraphs, still more is due to that simple and happy specific of unbinding the arm of British enterprise, which formerly we kept in fetters, and allowing it fair play in the general competition of the world. But I think there is one point yet remaining, which, if possible, affords still clearer demonstration than any that I have quoted, and that is what has happened to our shipping. Now, if we compare what has happened to the shipping of this country with what has happened to shipping elsewhere, then, indeed, the results of that comparison are remarkable ; because, gentlemen, you may remember that when the discussions on the repeal of the Navigation Laws arose, it was contended, and contended with some truth—I felt it myself, for one—that the pressure of foreign protective and prohibitory laws upon our shipping is much severer than upon our goods, inasmuch as it often happens, for example, that the law of commerce requiring a cargo to be sent to a certain port in a British ship in free competition with a ship of the country to which that port belongs, that that same law would require, if human law permitted, that the next voyage should be from that port to some other port to which the law of the country does not permit the British ship to go at all, and from which it is excluded by an absolute prohibition, while its own ship is allowed to go to it. However, I need not enter into these details. It is admitted that in no case could competition be more severe. I believe in no case could it be so severe as in the case of the competition of British ships with foreign ships. Consequently, on the occasion of the repeal of the Navigation Laws, the whole Protectionist party of the country went into the deepest mourning, and they said in solemn tones—for they rose to higher flights than usual—and said it represented not protection only but patriotism, a word of which we have heard a good deal on some more recent occasions. They told us that the repeal of the Navigation Laws was the destruction of the wooden walls of old England, and meant neither more nor less, according to the favorite phrase, than her reduction to the rank of a third-rate Power. All you who are old enough—and I am happy to think some of you are not old enough—will recollect the appalling vaticinations which went forth "thick as the leaves in Vallombrosa" over

the whole of the country. But the result has been where the
competition was the sharpest there the prosperity has been the
most extraordinary—I might say, had it not been realized, in
fact almost incredible. The tonnage of Great Brittain in 1840
was 6,490,000 tons. That tonnage had risen in 1880 to
41,348,000 tons, or was multiplied more than sixfold.

Now, that is an enormous result, and that is a result not due
to railways, because the railways do not run over the sea. It is
due to British energy working without any other advantage
than that. And it is a serious advantage, especially in certain
states of the world. It may be that we have become the home
of the shipbuilding trade of the world. But as between nation
and nation, that is a very small matter. The shipbuilder of
the Clyde will build a ship for a man in Havre on the same
terms as he will build a ship for a man in Hull, and it will
cost him as much to send the ship round to Hull as it will for
him to send it round to Havre. Therefore, there is no facti-
tious advantage to account for this astonishing result.

But I have got something to explain that in my mind is a
most satisfactory, although it might be taken on the other side
of the objection. I do not at all mean to say that our ships are
more than six times the bulk in 1880 than they were in 1840.
Not at all. They are nothing of the kind. The reports that
I have given to you are the reports founded upon clearances
inward and outward. They are the measures of the actual
tonnage employed in doing actual work. It is quite true we
have not got six times the capital involved in the fabrics of
ships. What does that mean? What will be your reply? So
much the better. With the smaller capital involved you are
doing a greater work. We are doing six times the work and
six times the amount of tonnage, because of the employment
of steam, of larger vessels, and of better machinery on board,
but with nothing approaching an increase of six times the
number of seamen, and doing the work, moreover, which six
times the number of seamen alone could, under the old methods of navigation, have pursued, and that is not owing to railways: that is owing to the effect of freedom, combined with
the remarkable advantages which have been gained by chang-

ing from wooden to iron shipbuilding in the conduct of the commerce of the world.

And now, gentlemen, what is the state of the case with regard to protected countries? There is a great bugbear that is continually paraded before us—the bugbear of the United States. And what has become of the shipping of the United States, and what has become of that shipping in its competition with British shipping? That shipping competes with British shipping not only upon equal and upon favored terms, for this reason—when a British ship goes from hence to America, goes from hence, say, to New York, to Boston, or to New Orleans, and then has got to make its next step, it has not got a free choice of the ports of the world. It cannot sail round upon what the Americans call the coasting trade, round Cape Horn to San Francisco. The British ship cannot, but the American ship may, consequently the British ship carrying cargo to America has a smaller choice, and, therefore, a restricted advantage. I only say that to show you that there is an inequality of law in the competition which is entirely against the British ships, and in favor of American ships. Gentlemen, my boyhood was spent at the mouth of the Mersey, and in those days I used to see those beautiful American liners, the packets between New York and Liverpool, which then conducted the bulk and the pick of the trade between the two countries. The Americans were deemed to be so entirely superior to us in shipbuilding and navigation that they had four-fifths of the whole trade between the two countries in their hands, and that four-fifths was the best of the trade ; and but the dregs were left in comparison to the one-fifth, the British shipping that entered into it. What is the case now when Free Trade has operated, and has applied its stimulus to the intelligence of England, and when on the other hand the action of the Americans has been restrained by the enactment, the enhancement, and the tightening of the protective system? The case is now that the scales are exactly reversed, and instead of America doing four-fifths, and that the best, we do four-fifths of the business, and that the best, and the Americans pick up, if I may so say, the leavings of the British and transact the residue of the trade. Not because they are inferior to us in anything ; it would be a fatal error to suppose it ; not because they have less intelligence, or because they have less perseverance. They are your descendants : they are your kinsmen ; and they are fully equal to you in all that goes to make human energy and power, but they are laboring under the delusion from which you yourselves have but recently escaped, and in which some misguided fellow-citizens seek again to entangle you. In 1850—I think I am right in saying that in 1850 the relative percentages of America and England in the sea trade of the world were represented by 15 for America and 41 for England. In the sea trade of the world, in 1880, the 41 of England had grown to 49, and the 15 of America had dwindled down to 6. There, gentlemen, are the genuine effects of a protective system exhibited before you, mitigated in the case of America by its own internal energies, and the enormous field that is open to them—a field which in your case you would not find, were you unhappily disposed to follow America in her errors. And the last word I will say to you is this, in the way of statistical statement : of the whole sea trade of the world, the 35,000,000 inhabiting these islands possess 52 per cent., more than one-half of the entire sea trade carried on by the entire human race, civilized or uncivilized. And yet so unthankful are we for the blessings we enjoy, and so unmindful of the dangers we have escaped, and the damages we have long suffered, that there are still many who go to British constituencies to invite them deliberately to march back from light into darkness, people who vainly and idly persuade themselves that if they are only sufficiently diligent and persevering they will convert their country to those pernicious notions.

Gentlemen. I have now fully satisfied what I think my duty on this matter in addressing to you a discourse that I admit, so far as you are concerned, is frivolous. It has been uninteresting to you. You knew it all before. I could tell you nothing you did not know. But some are not in the same happy condition. I hope that I have kept faithfully to the promise that I made that I should endeavor not to give a tinge of party to the discussion on which I have entered to-day, which yesterday I felt myself compelled to do. I hope I have faithfully observed that pledge ; and I shall conclude by expressing my belief that every man in this room sees the force of these facts and figures, however curtly and imperfectly stated. and my firm conviction that the people of this nation have now come to understand and to value the system of commercial freedom, and that they will maintain those beneficent and philanthropic and most fruitful laws as among the solid and permanent institutions of the country. fraught with blessings to every order of this community and to all the nations of the world.